Gifted and Test Prep 1

Geared For NNAT® and OLSAT®

For ages 3-6

2014 Edition

Publishing, Inc.
THE PATH TO ACHIEVING EXCELLENCE!

by **Jack and Jill Publishing, Inc.**

Luke Geraci

Stephanie Pang

Raymond Pang

Tommy Ng

Erik Zhao

Priscilla Wong

Patrick Nian

Matthew Rotlevi

Owen Pang

Carolyn Lau

Eric Morgenstern

Note: This book is a non-profit project. All profits will be donated to orphanages so that children all over may benefit from this book.

Gifted and Talented Test Prep 1
Geared for NNAT® and OLSAT®
for ages 3-6

Illustrated by: Jack and Jill Publishing Inc.
Written and Published by: Jack and Jill Publishing Inc.

All of the questions in this book were written by:

Luke Geraci	Patrick Nian
Stephanie Pang	Matthew Rotlevi
Raymond Pang	Owen Pang
Tommy Ng	Carolyn Lau
Erik Zhao	Eric Morgenstern
Priscilla Wong	

ISBN-13: 978-1490914046
ISBN-10: 1490914048

Jack and Jill Publishing Inc.
Queens, New York,
USA
Jack.jill.publishing@gmail.com

Dear Parents,

As a mother of four, I have realized the importance of education in children's lives. Early childhood education is particularly essential in that it provides the foundation that will guide students through all of their future learning experiences. Children who are deemed "gifted" are usually identified at relatively young ages, even though very few are likely to have been born with superior natural abilities. These children gradually excel in school and attain academic success by being exposed to the appropriate stimulation at an early age. I strongly believe that all children, not just a select few, are born with the natural intelligence needed to excel academically. However, some children may need an extra push to reach their full potential. My goal is to help encourage excellence in these children by providing parents with the right resources.

In some cases, exceptionally gifted children are enrolled in Gifted and Talented or Magnet programs and are provided with an opportunity to thrive in an enriched and/ or accelerated educational environment designed specifically for students at their level. Programs like these often require an admissions exam to determine whether or not a student is academically eligible for enrollment. This book, which focuses on some basic skills including critical thinking, math, and problem-solving, is intended to help students prepare for the OLSAT (Otis-Lennon School Ability Test) and other similar screening tests.

I wish you the best of luck on this wonderful and rewarding journey of watching your child expand their knowledge and discover new things about themselves.

Sincerely,

Priscilla Wong

Note: The OLSAT was created by Dr. Arthur Otis in 1918 at Stanford University to measure students' ability to perform school learning tasks and to determine their placement for school programs. The latest OLSAT is used in several educational systems in the United States of America. In New York, the OLSAT is used along with the Naglieri Nonverbal Ability Test (NNAT2) to determine admission into the District and Citywide Gifted and Talented Programs. In California, the Davis Unified School District administers the OLSAT in order to see whether students in Grades 3-8 qualify for the District Gifted and Talented Programs. In addition, the Greenwich Public Schools District Board of Education in Connecticut uses the OLSAT alongside the Stanford Achievement Test to check the performance of children in the 3rd, 5th, and 7th grades.

First Day of School

One early ☀ morning, Jack and Jill were sleeping. Their puppy Billy and their kitten Bella jumped on their beds "Bark! Bark! ..." "Meow! Meow! ..." Jack and Jill's mom walked into their room and said, "Today is the first day of school! Wake up! Wake up!" Jack and Jill ate breakfast quickly and hurried to put on their book bags. Mom helped Jill to tie her shoelaces while Billy waited by the door. A bird flew by them as they walked to the bus stop. The yellow school bus came to drive them to school. Jack and Jill met new friends on the playground and learned all about different shapes, colors and animals in the classroom.

Table of Contents

Billy only likes to lie on  red square mats.
Circle/point to all the places where Billy likes to lie down.

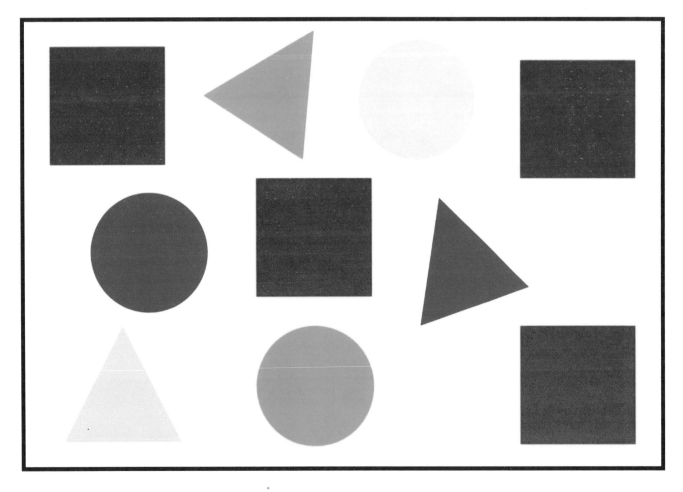

The wind blew away all of Jill's mail! They are ▓ blue squares. Circle/point to all the blue squares to help Jill find her mail.

Jack and Jill need to help their teacher decorate the classroom with   yellow squares. Circle/point to all the yellow squares to help them decorate!

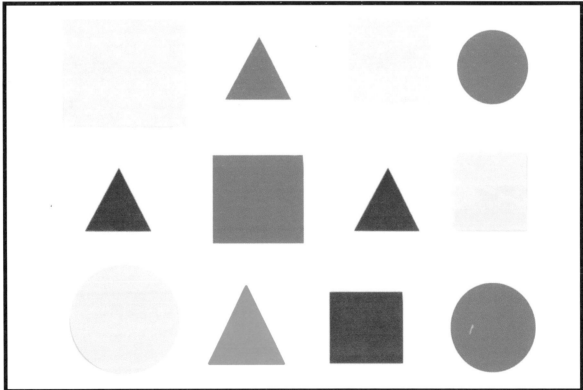

Find two blue triangles  to make Jack's balance beam the same on both sides.

Jack and Jill are putting together a puzzle but they are still missing 2  yellow triangles. Can you help them find the last two pieces?

Jill has cut out many red circles  like the one she is holding for a school work. Can you circle/point to all the red circles in the picture below that Jill cut out?

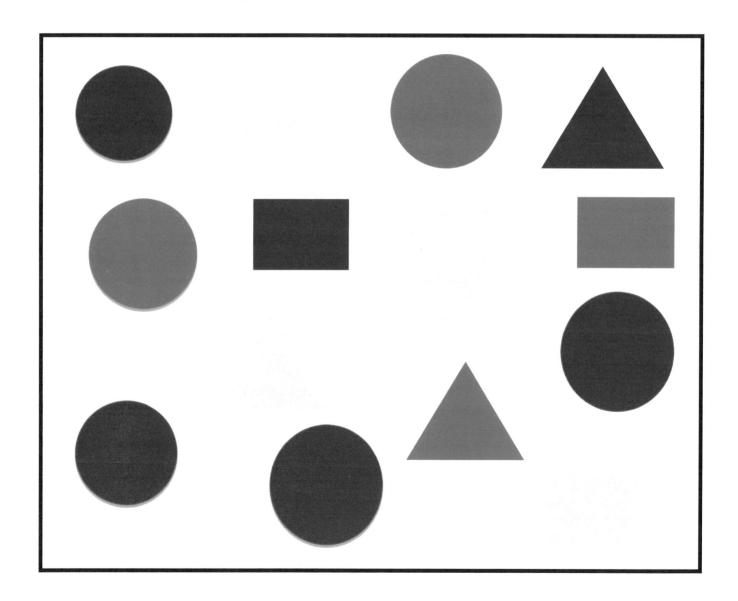

Jack has a puppy named Billy who is lost and needs to find his way back to Jack. However, Billy only follows blue circles. Draw a line connecting all the blue circles to make a path that leads Billy back to Jack.

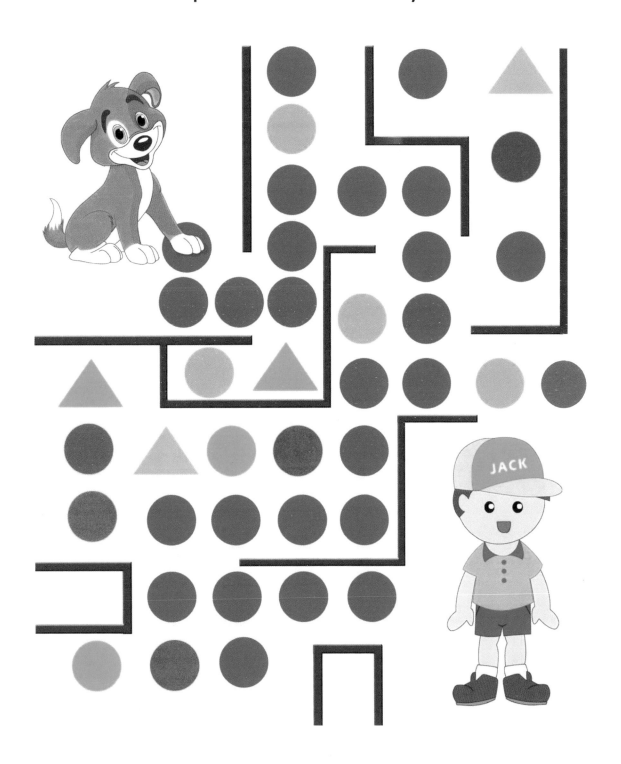

Jack and Jill need to set the table, but they have to use only yellow circle   placemats. Circle/point to all the placemats on the table that Jack and Jill should use.

1. Circle/point to the two red suns.

2. Circle/point to the two blue flowers.

3. Circle/point to the two yellow lollipops.

Find and circle the picture that shows a river in between two houses. One house is red and the other one is yellow.

Draw lines to connect pairs of identical figures.

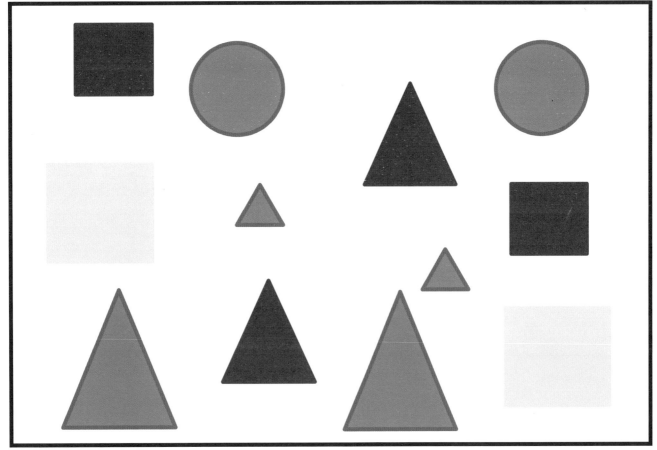

What do you need to play each sport? Draw a line to connect each sport equipment to the correct ball.

1.

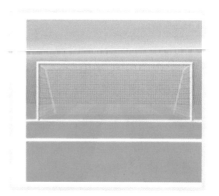

2.

3.

4.

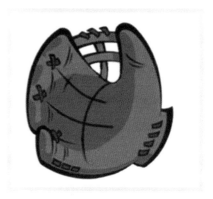

Draw lines to connect the things that belong together.

5.

6.

7.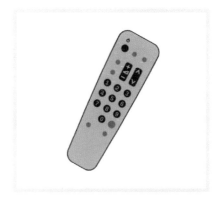

8.

Draw lines to connect each food to their related object.

9.

10.

11.

12.

Draw lines to connect each school supply to the object that has the same function.

13.

 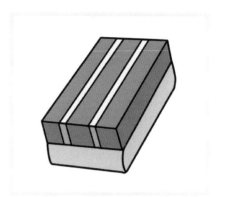

14.

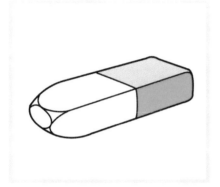 

15.

16.

Draw lines to connect things that belong in the same group.

17.

18.

19.

20.

21. Choose the 4 pictures in the outer purple circles that best relate to the picture in the inner yellow circle and draw lines to connect them.

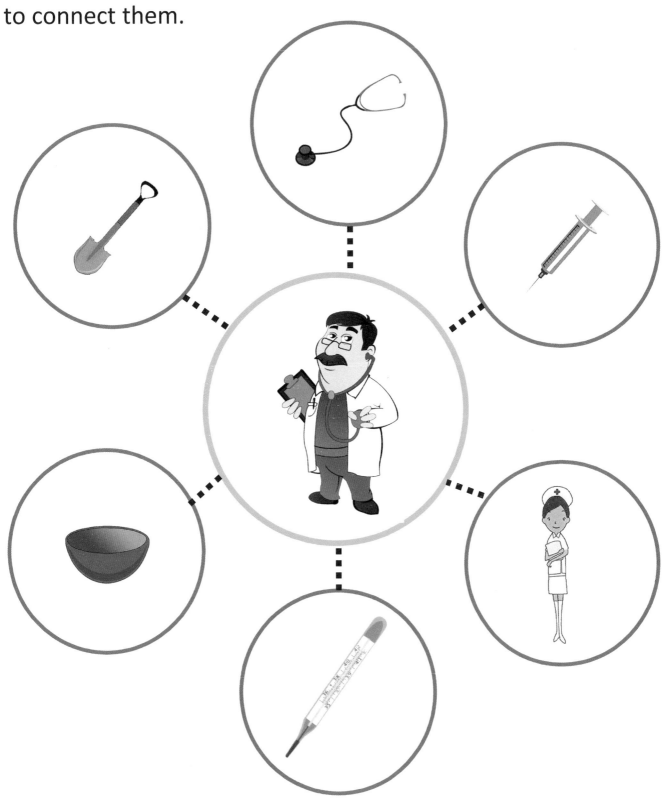

22. Choose the 4 pictures in the outer purple circles that best relate to the picture in the inner yellow circle and draw lines to connect them.

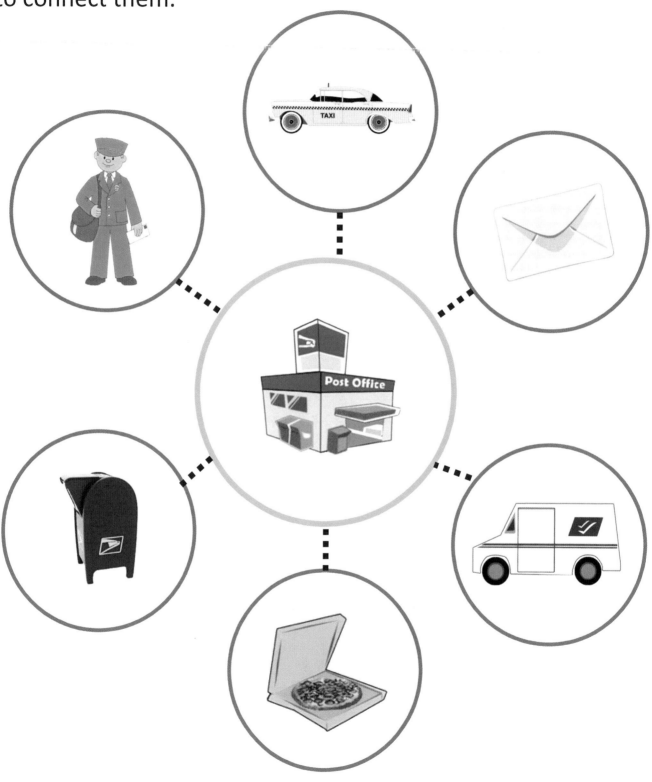

23. Choose the 4 pictures in the outer purple circles that best relate to the picture in the inner yellow circle and draw lines to connect them.

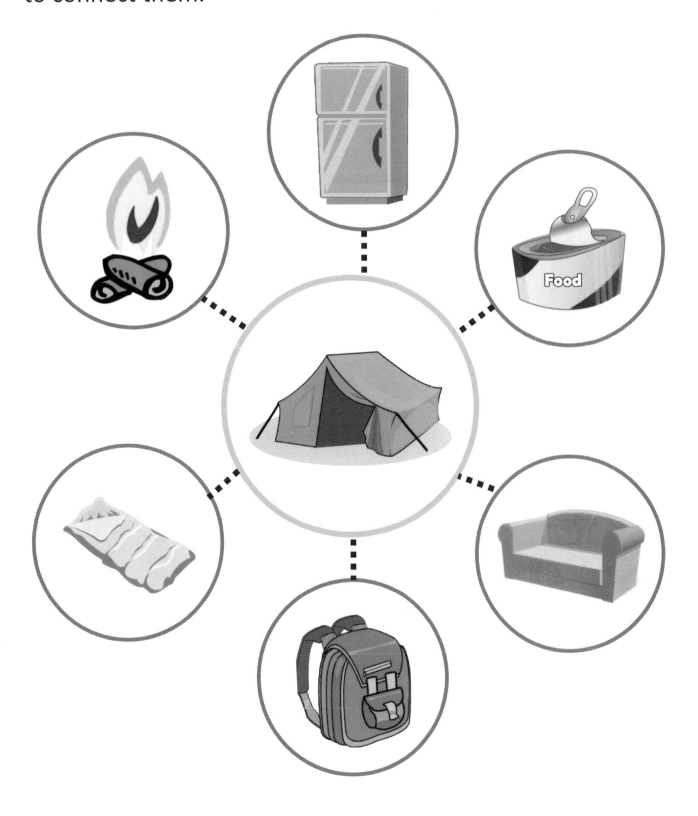

24. Choose the 4 pictures in the outer purple circles that best relate to the picture in the inner yellow circle and draw lines to connect them.

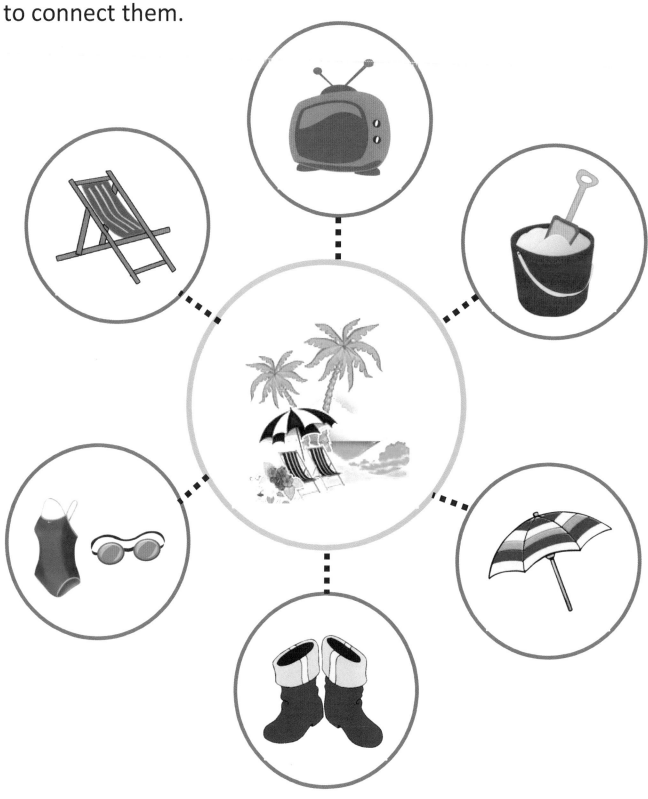

Fill in the circle under the picture that will complete the pattern.

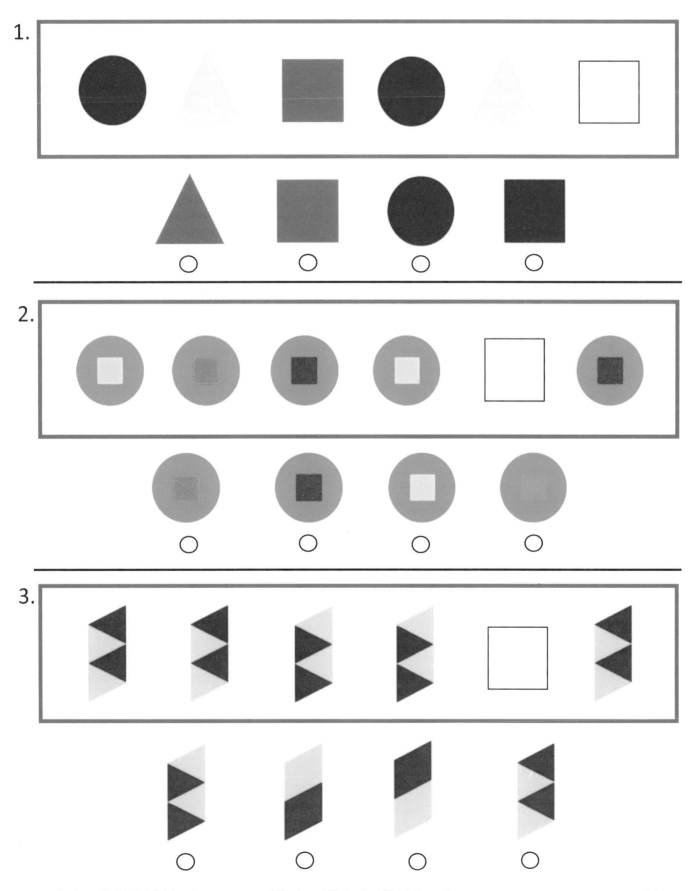

Fill in the circle under the picture that will complete the pattern.

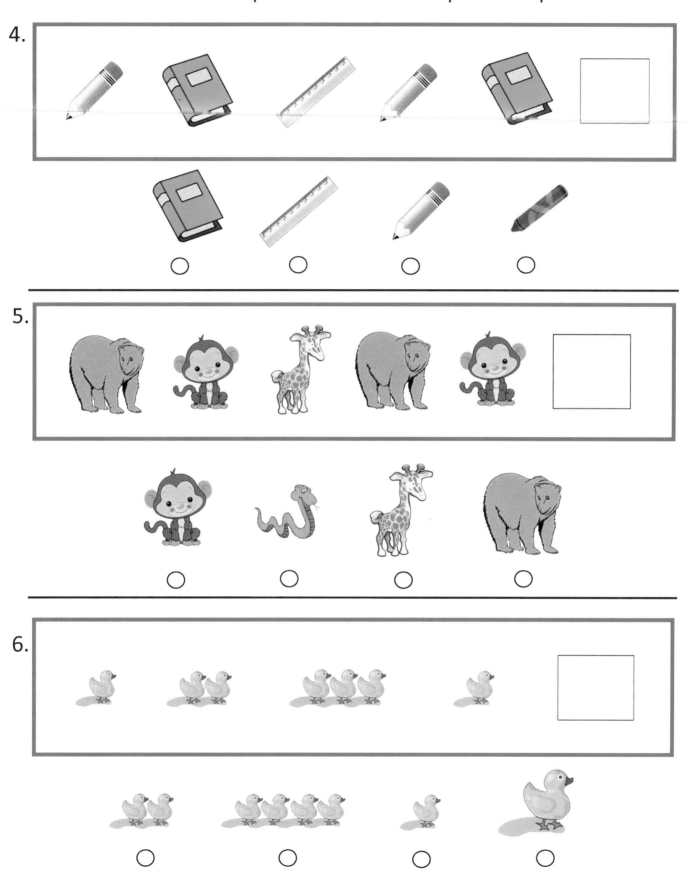

Fill in the circle under the picture that will complete the pattern.

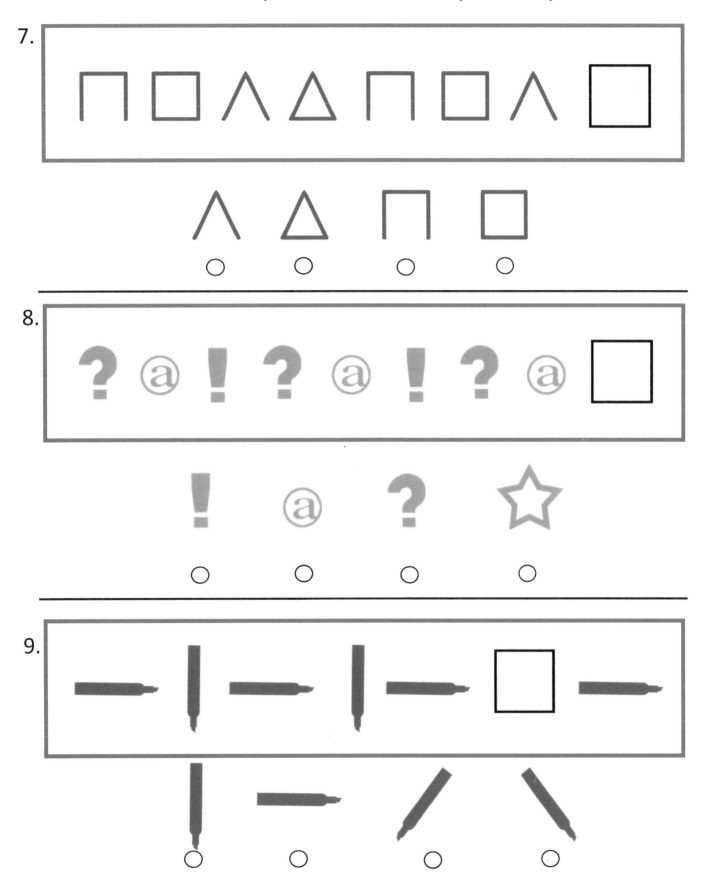

Fill in the circle under the picture that will complete the pattern.

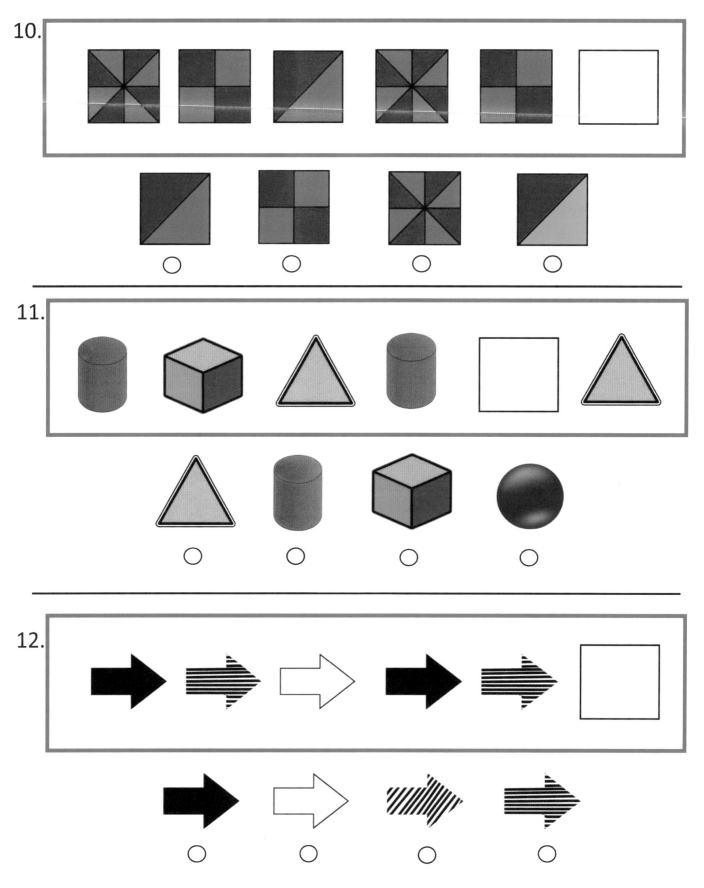

Fill in the circle under the picture that will complete the pattern.

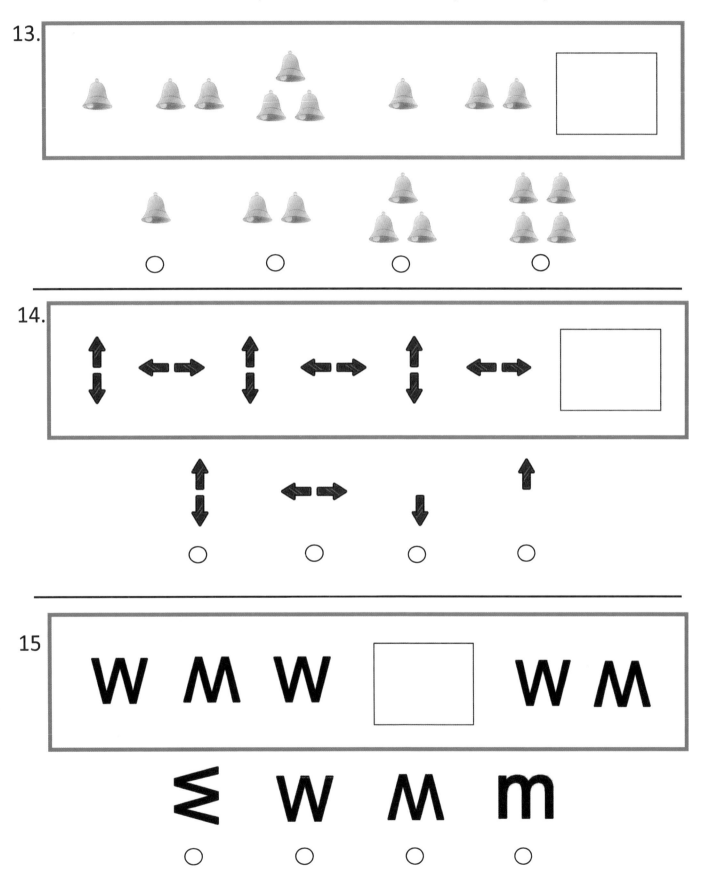

13.

14.

15.

Fill in the circle under the picture that will complete the pattern.

16.

A<small>V</small>   B<small>V</small>   C<small>V</small>   D<small>V</small>

A<small>V</small>   D<small>V</small>   E<small>V</small>   F<small>V</small>
 ○   ○   ○   ○

17.

18.

Fill in the circle under the picture that will complete the pattern.

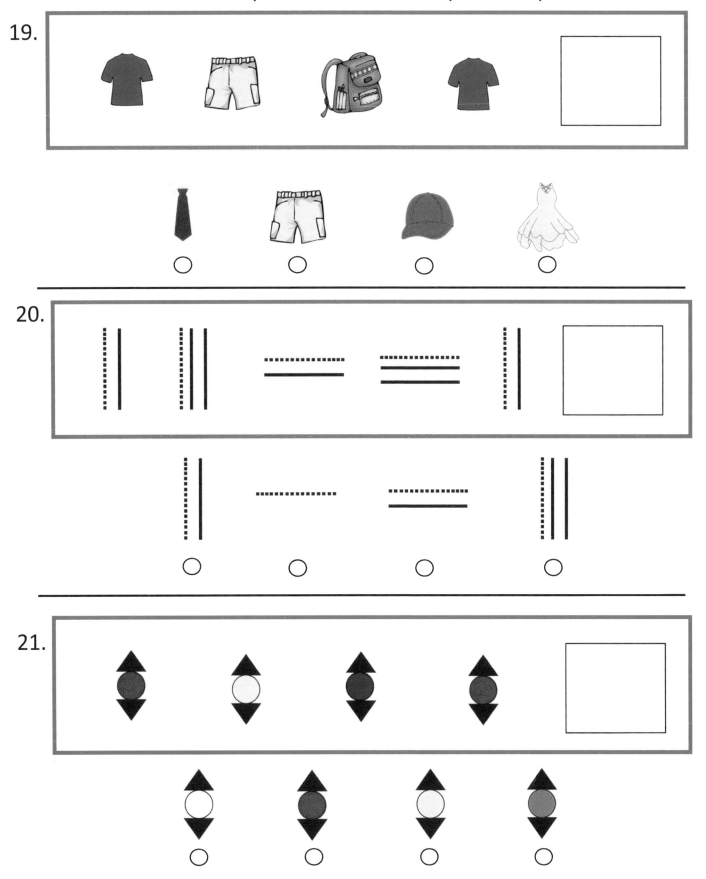

Fill in the circle under the picture that will complete the pattern.

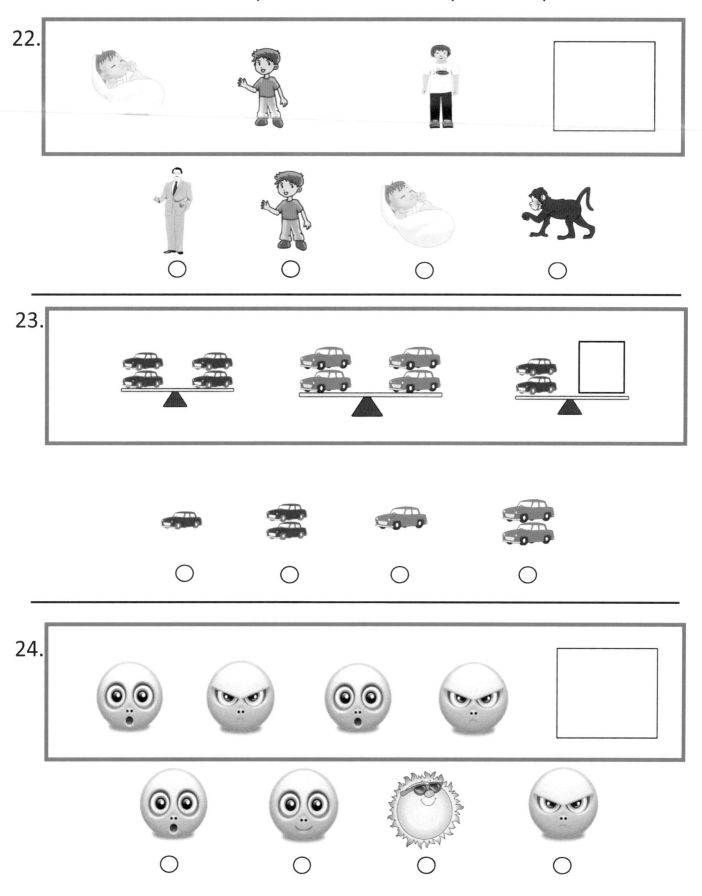

1. Fill in the circle under the picture that has 3 stars.

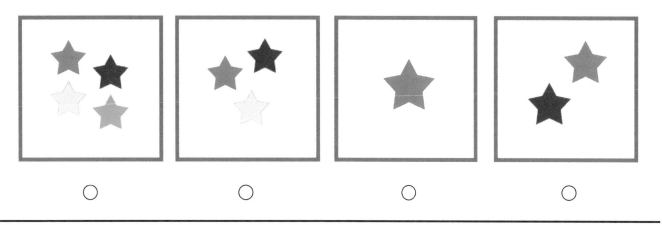

2. Fill in the circle under the picture that has 5 ice cream cones.

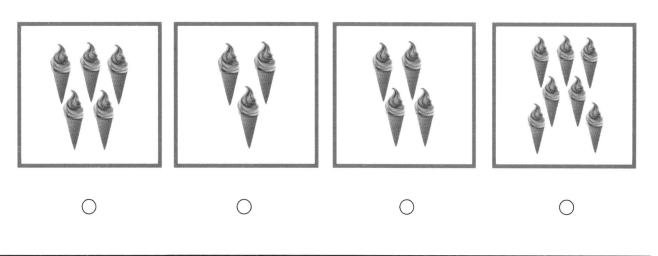

3. Fill in the circle under the picture that has 2 cars.

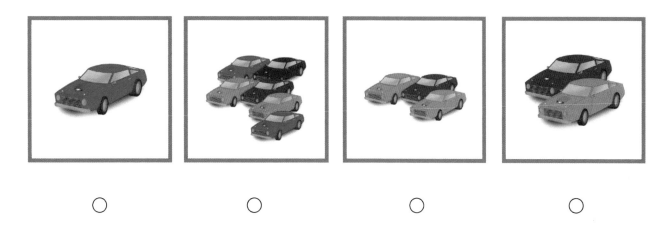

4. Jack is playing with blocks. How many blocks does he have?

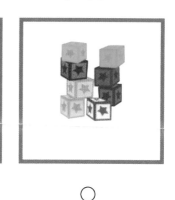

○   ○   ○

5. Jill needs to buy eggs. How many eggs are in her carton?

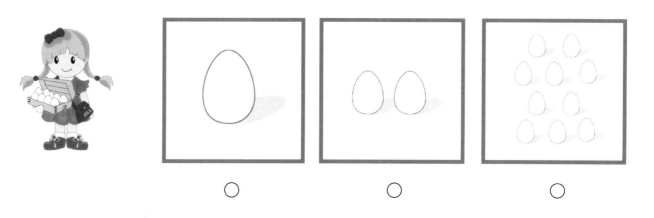

○   ○   ○

6. How many dogs are playing?

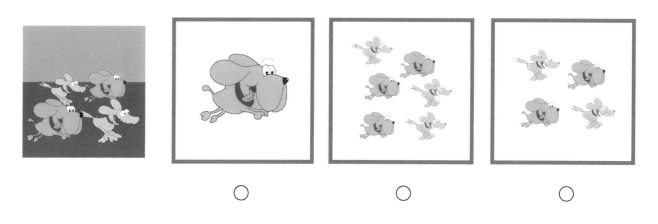

○   ○   ○

7. How many kites are flying in the sky?

  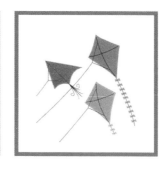 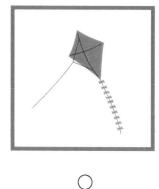

                      ○   ○   ○

8. How many fish are in the tank?

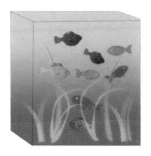   

                      ○   ○   ○

9. How many flowers are growing in the garden?

                      ○   ○   ○

Look at this picture and answer the questions below.

10. How many  cats are there?

11. How many  crayons are there?

12. How many  pictures are there?

Look at this picture and answer the questions below.

13. How many  buckets are there?

14. How many  shovels are there?

15. How many  balls are there?

Look at this picture and answer the questions below.

16. How many  puppies are there?

17. How many  ducks are there?

18. How many  birds are there?

Look at this picture and answer the questions below.

19. How many  cows are there?

20. How many  chickens are there?

21. How many  apples are there?

Look at this picture and answer the questions below.

22. How many  worms are there?

23. How many  birds are there?

24. How many  eggs are there?

Circle the two pictures that are exactly the same.

1.

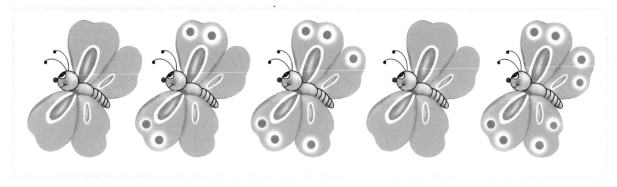

2.

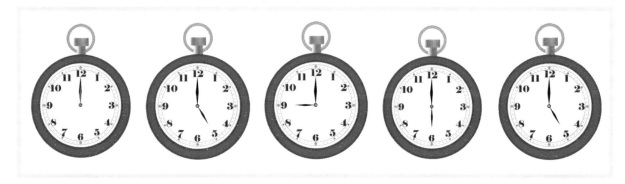

3.

Circle the two pictures that are exactly the same.

4.

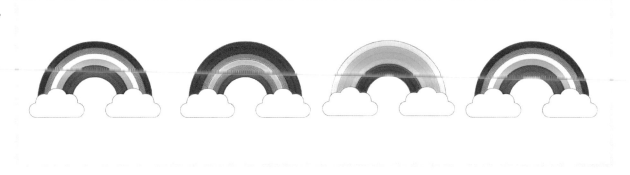

5.

6.

Circle the two pictures that are exactly the same.

7.

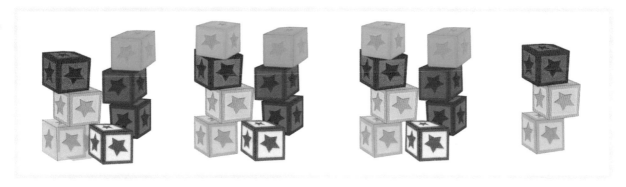

8.

9.

Here you see a pattern in each row. Continue the pattern by drawing the picture that comes next.

10.

11.

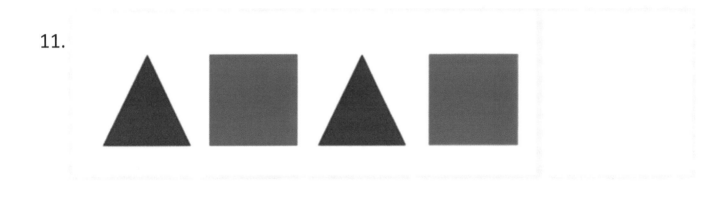

12.

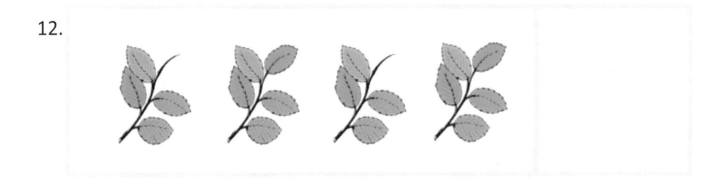

Here you see a pattern in each row. Continue the pattern by drawing the number that comes next.

13.

14.

15.

1. Which picture shows a car in front of a garbage can?

2. Which picture shows two bees on the top of a flower?

3. Which picture shows a mouse on top of a table while another below the table?

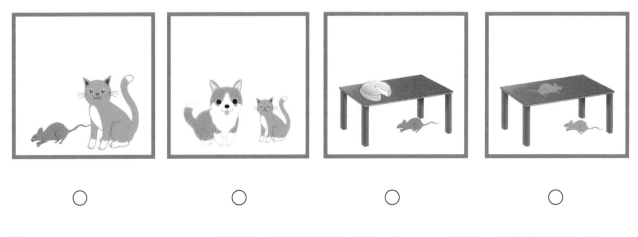

4. Which picture shows 3 ducks in a lake and a fox behind a tree?

    ○   ○   ○   ○

5. Which picture shows a dog under a chair?

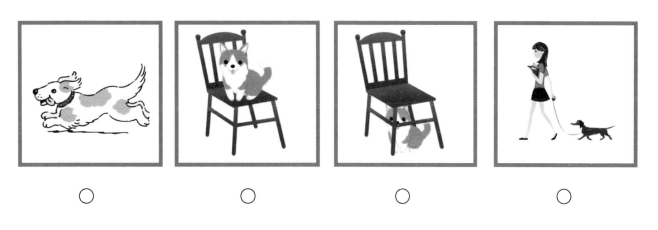

    ○   ○   ○   ○

6. Which picture shows a baby next to a toy car?

    ○   ○   ○   ○

7. Which picture shows two arrows pointing toward each other?

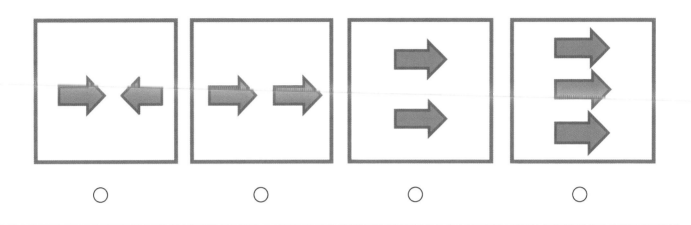

○   ○   ○   ○

8. Which picture shows a triangle on top of a square?

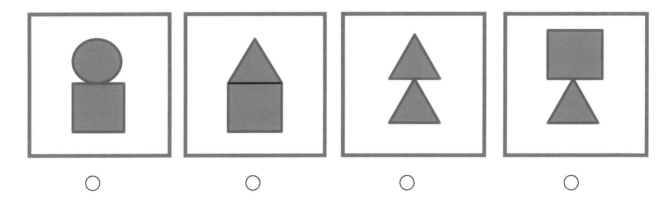

○   ○   ○   ○

9. Which picture shows a star inside a circle?

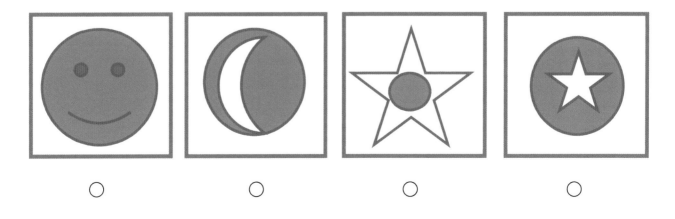

○   ○   ○   ○

Look at the picture below and answer the questions that follow.

10. Circle the dog on top of a garbage can.

11. Circle the bird in front of a kite.

12. Circle the cat behind a tree.

13. Circle the man sitting next to Jack.

Look at the picture below and answer the questions that follow.

14. Circle an egg that is inside an egg carton.

15. Circle the carton of eggs that is between two bottles of strawberry jam.

16. Circle the bottle of milk that is next to the jar of peanut butter.

17. Circle the apple that is to the left of the watermelon.

Look at the picture below and answer the questions that follow.

18. Circle the picture that is to the left of the picture with the blue frame.

19. Circle the stuffed animal that is next to the horse.

20. Circle the toy car that is between two red toy cars.

21. Circle the red block that is between two yellow blocks.

For each of the questions below, you will see four colored boxes. Circle the picture from the right that belongs in the empty box so that the red boxes go together in the same way that the pictures in the blue boxes do.

1.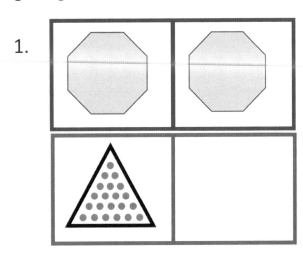

1    2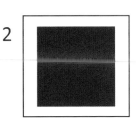

3    4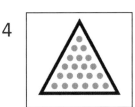

2.

1    2

3    4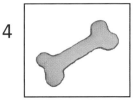

3.

1    2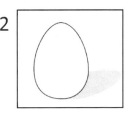

3    4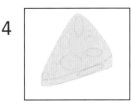

For each of the questions below, you will see four colored boxes. Circle the picture from the right that belongs in the empty box so that the red boxes go together in the same way that the pictures in the blue boxes do.

4.

5.

6.

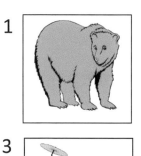

For each of the questions below, you will see four colored boxes. Circle the picture from the right that belongs in the empty box so that the red boxes go together in the same way that the pictures in the blue boxes do.

7.

          1    2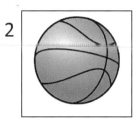

          3    4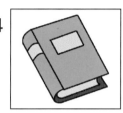

8.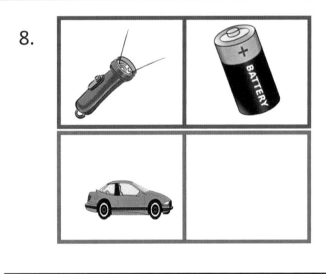

          1 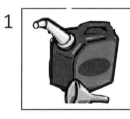   2

          3 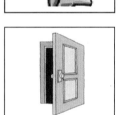   4

9.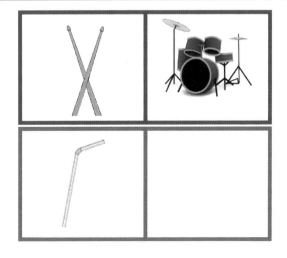

          1    2

          3    4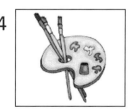

For each of the questions below, you will see four colored boxes. Circle the picture from the right that belongs in the empty box so that the red boxes go together in the same way that the pictures in the blue boxes do.

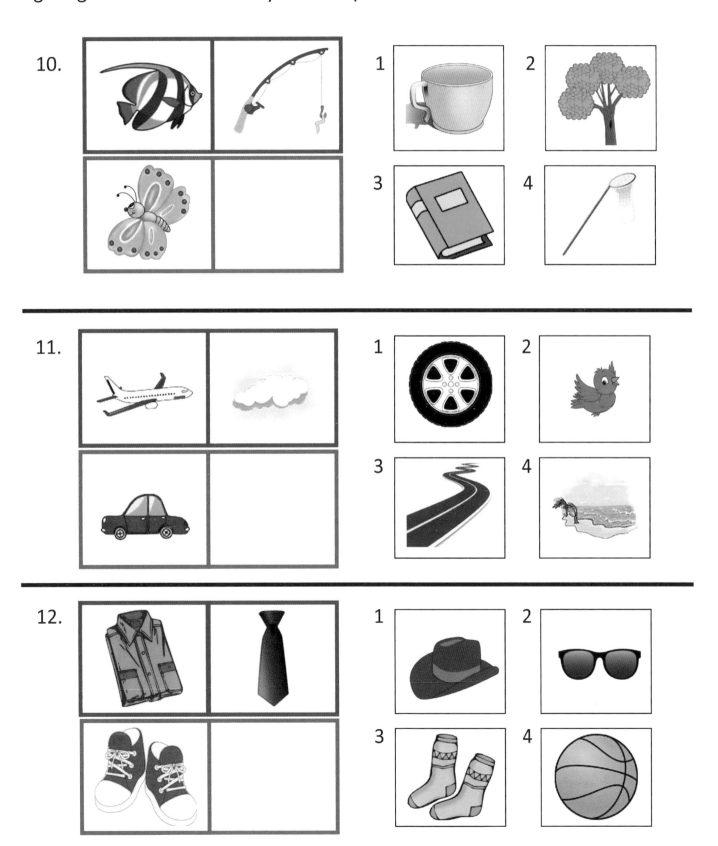

For each of the questions below, you will see four colored boxes. Circle the picture from the right that belongs in the empty box so that the red boxes go together in the same way that the pictures in the blue boxes do.

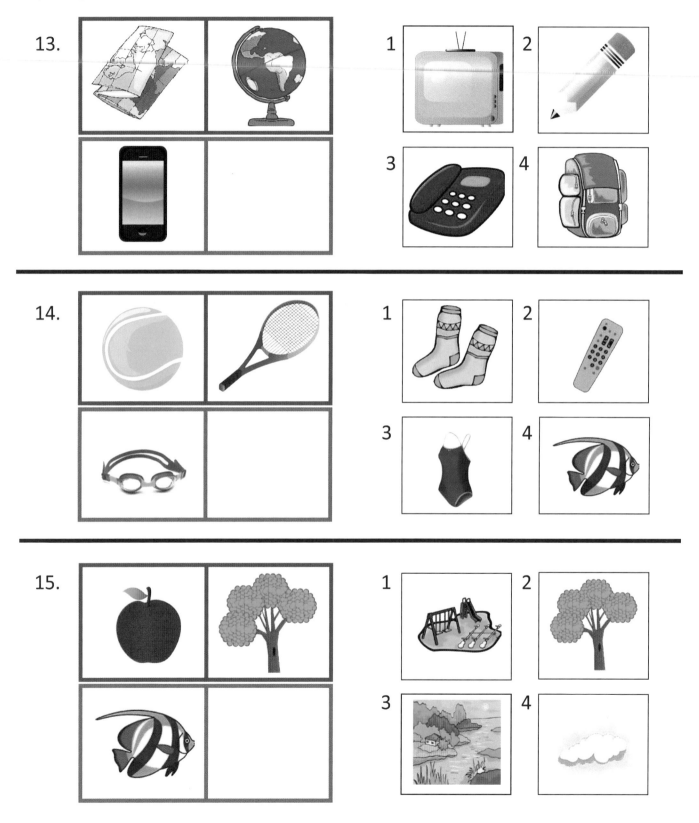

For each of the questions below, you will see four colored boxes. Circle the picture from the right that belongs in the empty box so that the red boxes go together in the same way that the pictures in the blue boxes do.

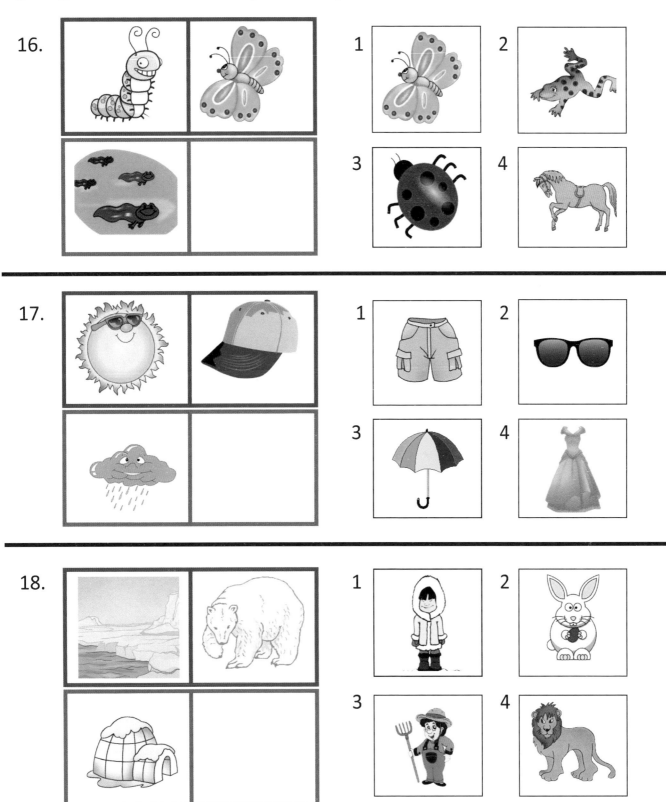

For each of the questions below, you will see four colored boxes. Circle the picture from the right that belongs in the empty box so that the red boxes go together in the same way that the pictures in the blue boxes do.

19.

20.

21.

For each of the questions below, you will see four colored boxes. Circle the picture from the right that belongs in the empty box so that the red boxes go together in the same way that the pictures in the blue boxes do.

22.

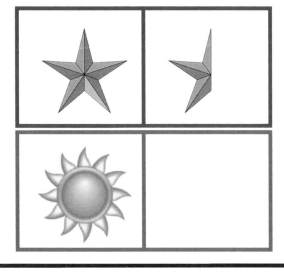

1    2

3    4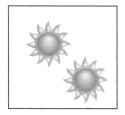

23.

1    2

3    4

24.

1    2

3   4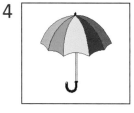

Fill in the circle under the picture that does not belong.

1.

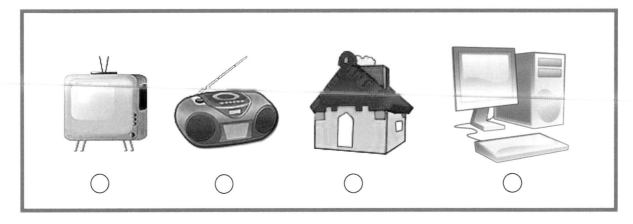

○   ○   ○   ○

2.

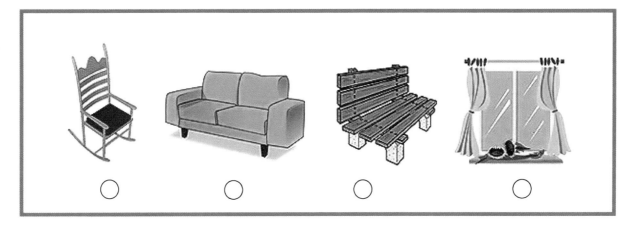

○   ○   ○   ○

3.

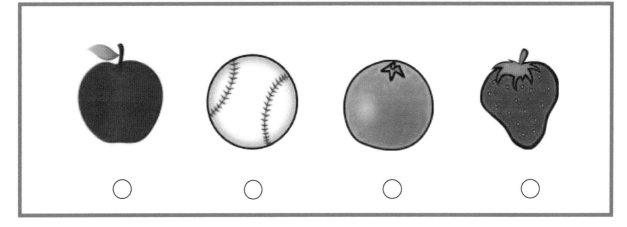

○   ○   ○   ○

Fill in the circle under the picture that does not belong.

4.

○   ○   ○   ○

5.

○   ○   ○   ○

6.

○   ○   ○   ○

Fill in the circle under the picture that does not belong.

7.

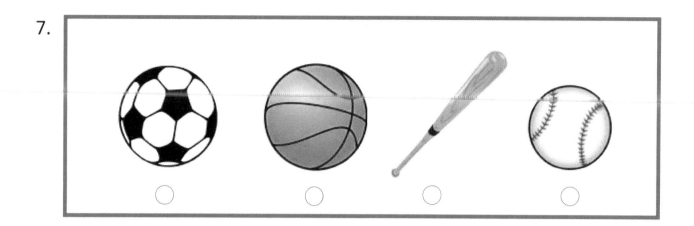

8.

9.

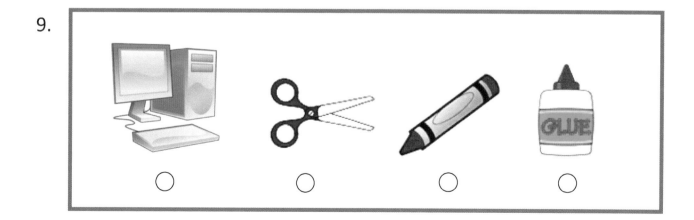

Gifted and Talented Test Prep 1

Jack and Jill Publishing Inc.

Fill in the circle under the picture that does not belong.

10.

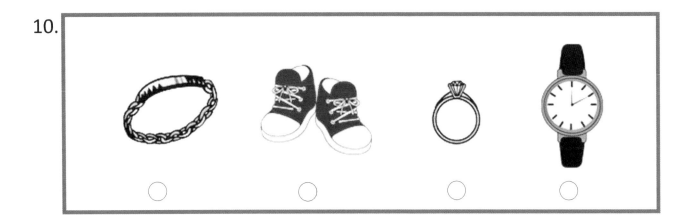

○   ○   ○   ○

11.

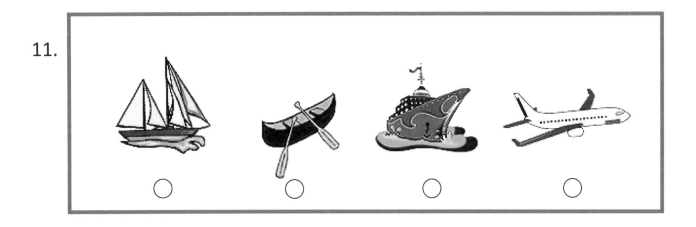

○   ○   ○   ○

12.

○   ○   ○   ○

Fill in the circle under the picture that does not belong.

13.

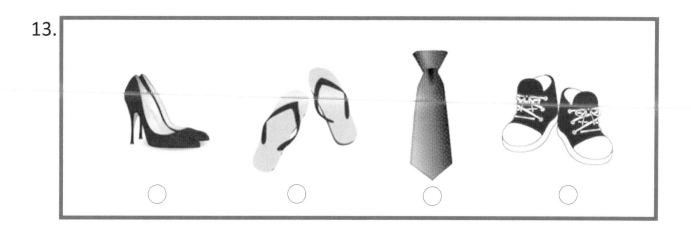

14.

15.

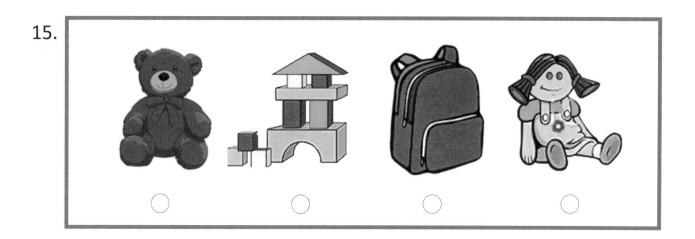

Fill in the circle under the picture that does not belong.

16.

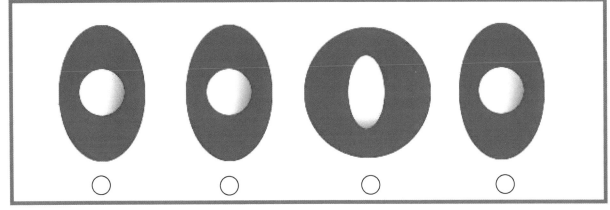

○   ○   ○   ○

17.

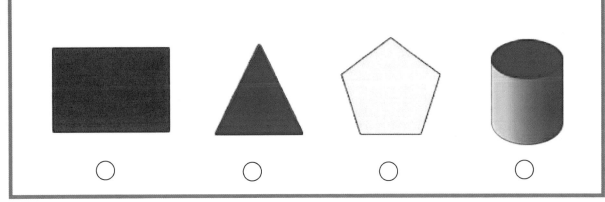

○   ○   ○   ○

18.

○   ○   ○   ○

Choose the picture that goes best with the picture in the first box.

1.

⚪   ⚪   ⚪

2.

⚪   ⚪   ⚪

3.

⚪   ⚪   ⚪

Choose the picture that goes best with the picture in the first box.

4.

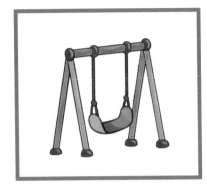 

◯   ◯   ◯

5.

◯   ◯   ◯

6.

 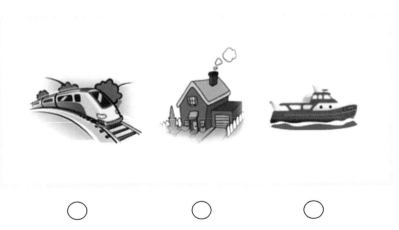

◯   ◯   ◯

Choose the picture that goes best with the picture in the first box.

7.

○   ○   ○

8.

○   ○   ○

9.

○   ○   ○

Choose the picture that goes best with the picture in the first box.

10.

      ○

11.

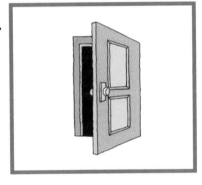  

      ○

12.

      ○

Choose the picture that goes best with the picture in the first box.

7.          

8.          

9.       

Choose the picture that goes best with the picture in the first box.

10.
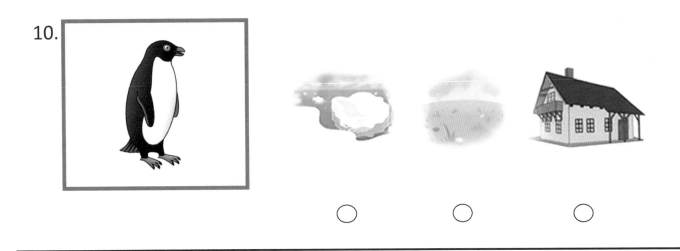

11.
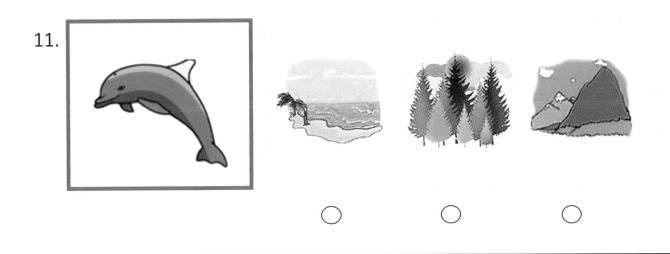

12.

1. Number the pictures or draw a line connecting the pictures in the order that they happen.

3. Number the pictures or draw a line connecting the pictures in the order that they happen.

2. Number the pictures or draw a line connecting the pictures in the order that they happen.

4. Number the pictures or draw a line connecting the pictures in the order that they happen.

5. Number the pictures or draw a line connecting the pictures in the order that they happen.

Additional NNAT Exercise

Note to parents: The following pages are practice NNAT nonverbal questions designed to model actual questions from the NNAT. There is no time limit for these practice questions, but it is recommended that students complete these questions on their own without any distractions around them. Students may see the pictures below for an example.

1

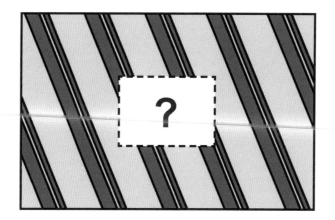

    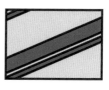

①   ②   ③   ④   ⑤

2

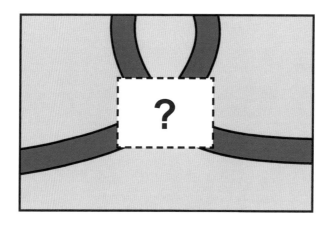

 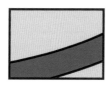 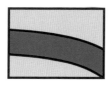 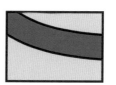 

①   ②   ③   ④   ⑤

3

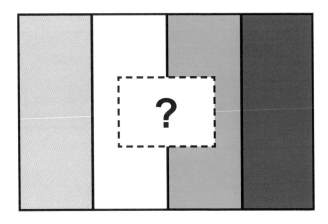

① 　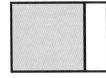
② 　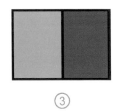
③ 　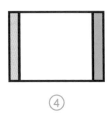
④ 　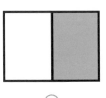
⑤

4

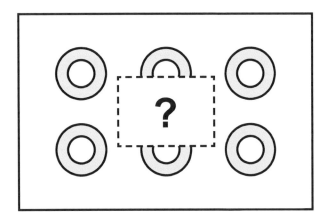

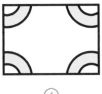
① 　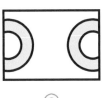
② 　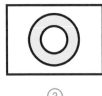
③ 　
④ 　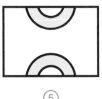
⑤

5

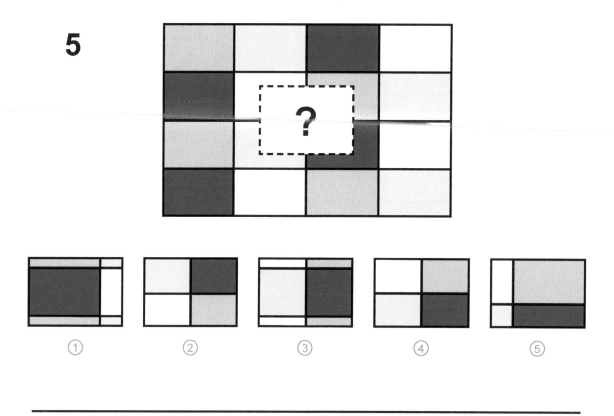

6

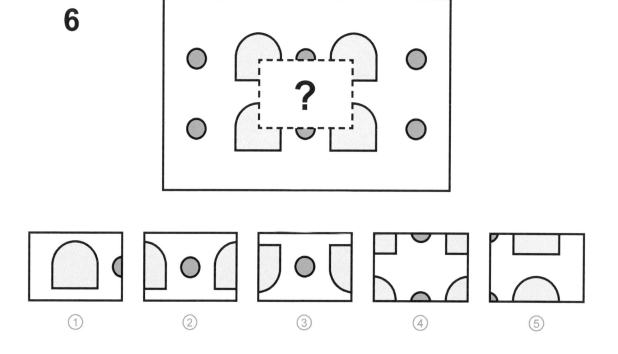

Gifted and Talented Test Prep 1 Jack and Jill Publishing Inc.

7

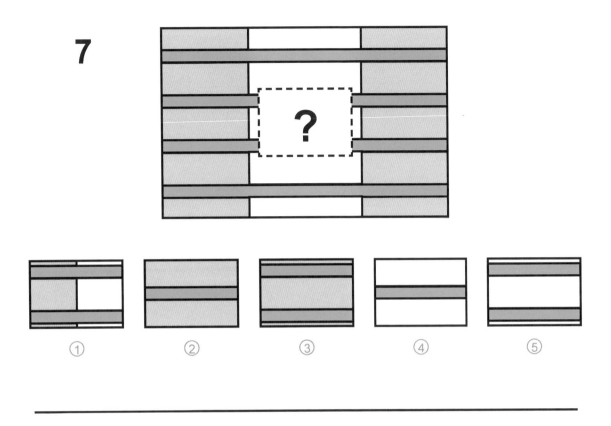

8

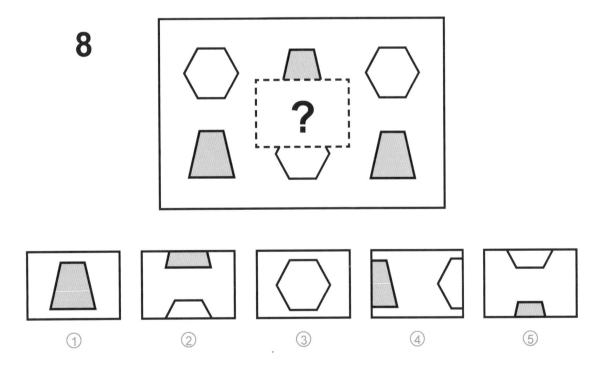

9

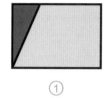  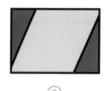 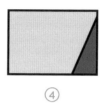 

① ② ③ ④ ⑤

10

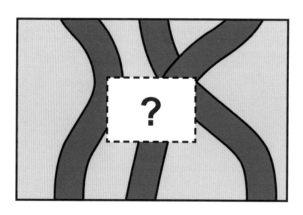

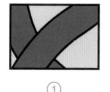  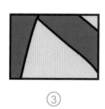  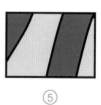

① ② ③ ④ ⑤

Gifted and Talented Test Prep 1 Jack and Jill Publishing Inc.

11

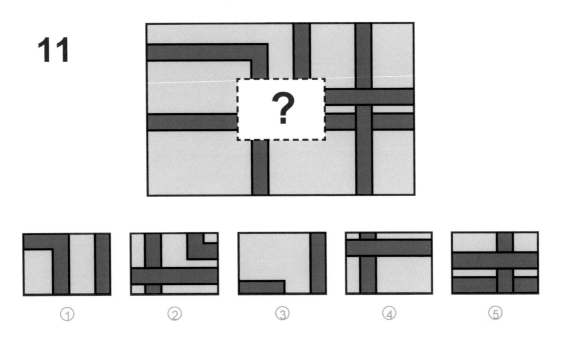

① ② ③ ④ ⑤

12

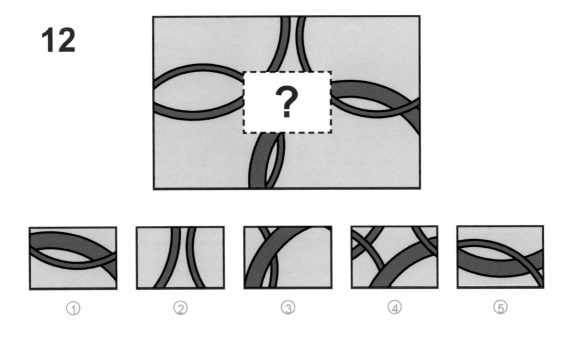

① ② ③ ④ ⑤

13

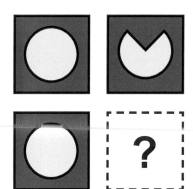

①   ②   ③   ④   ⑤

14

①   ②   ③   ④   ⑤

Gifted and Talented Test Prep 1   Jack and Jill Publishing Inc.

15

① ② ③ ④ ⑤

16

① ② ③ ④ ⑤

17

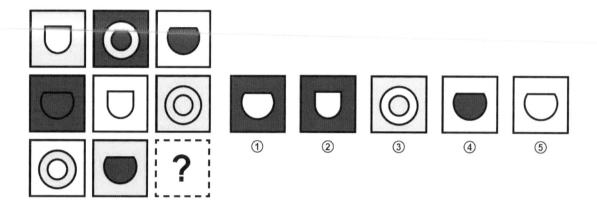

18

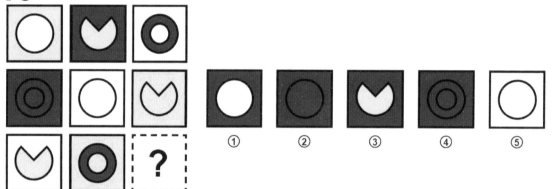

19

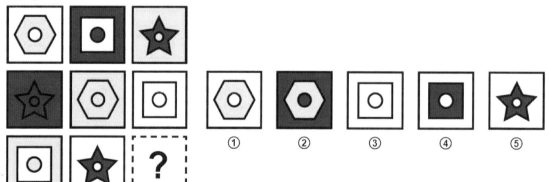

Gifted and Talented Test Prep 1   Jack and Jill Publishing Inc.

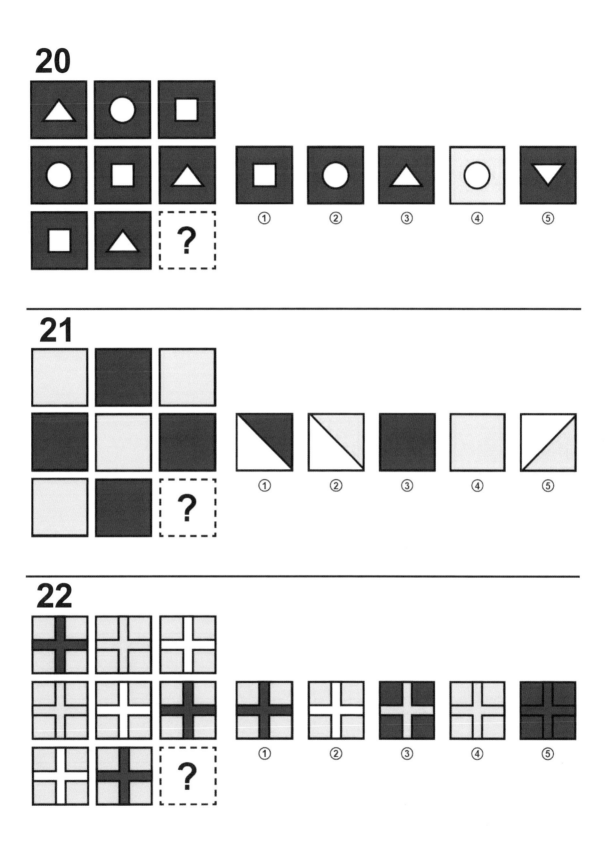

20

21

22

23

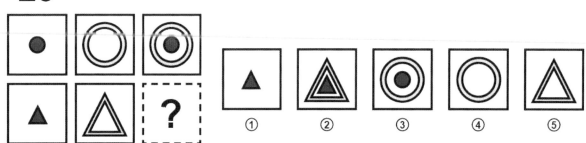

24

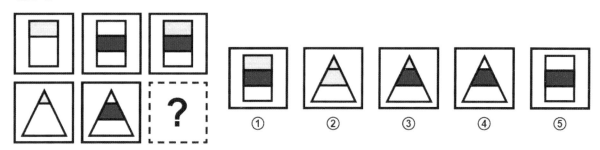

25

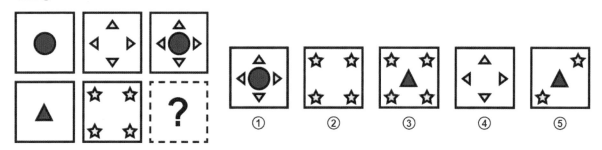

Before beginning the test:
- Tear out the test prompts/instructions and answers. (Pages 96-101)
- Seat the child at a table with the practice test and a pencil.
- Remove all other distractions and inform the child that he/she will be taking a test today.

During the test:
- Maintain a relaxed environment. Do not stress the child out during the test.
- Keep in mind that these 30 questions are to be done within **30 minutes**. Each child should not take longer than 1 minutes for each question.
- Sit next to the child and read aloud the prompts below that are **bolded and blue.** Pause after each question and give time for the child to turn the page when necessary.

Scoring Guidelines
- Score the test by counting the total number of correct answers.
- When taking actual tests for gifted and talented programs, your child's score will most likely be scaled scores or percentile ranks which take into consideration other factors such as age or content.
- Please remember that these tests and scores do not indicate what your child will get in standardized gifted and talented tests and rather only serve as practice for the real exams. In fact, your child will most likely score higher on the actual tests than these practice tests.

OLSAT Practice Test

30 minutes

Parents: Before beginning, please tear out the pages 96-101 which are written in blue text and located directly behind this practice test for the prompts to read to your child as he/she takes this test and for the answers.

1.

2.

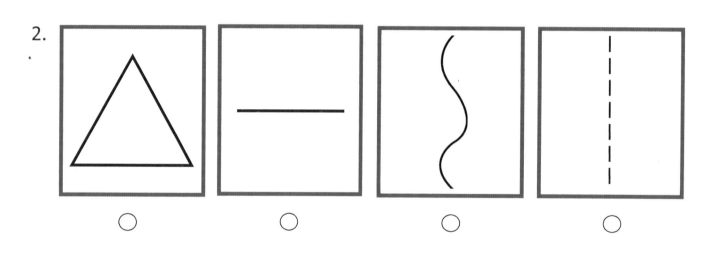

3.

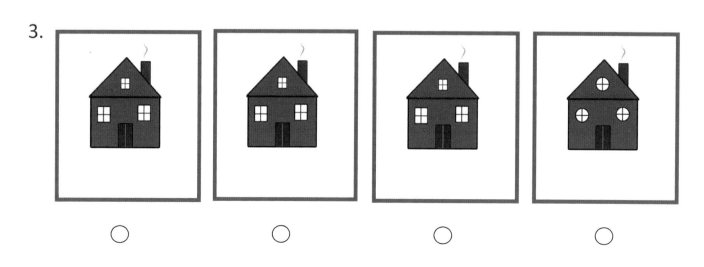

Gifted and Talented Test Prep 1

Jack and Jill Publishing Inc.

4.

○   ○   ○   ○

5.

○   ○   ○   ○

6.

○   ○   ○   ○

7.

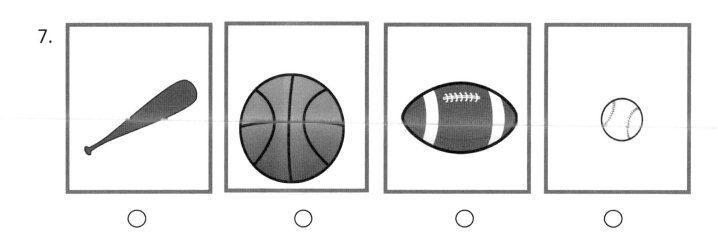

○   ○   ○   ○

8.

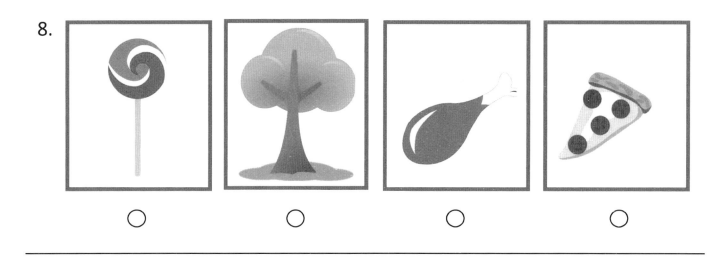

○   ○   ○   ○

9.

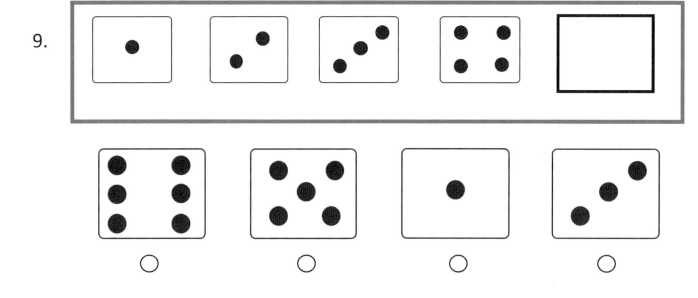

○   ○   ○   ○

10.

 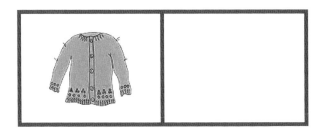

    ○   ○   ○   ○

11.

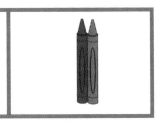 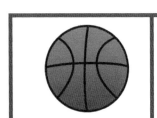

    ○   ○   ○   ○

12.

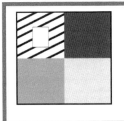    

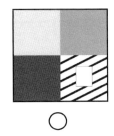 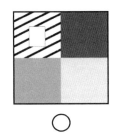 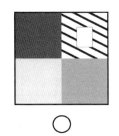 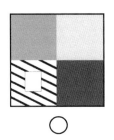

    ○   ○   ○   ○

13.

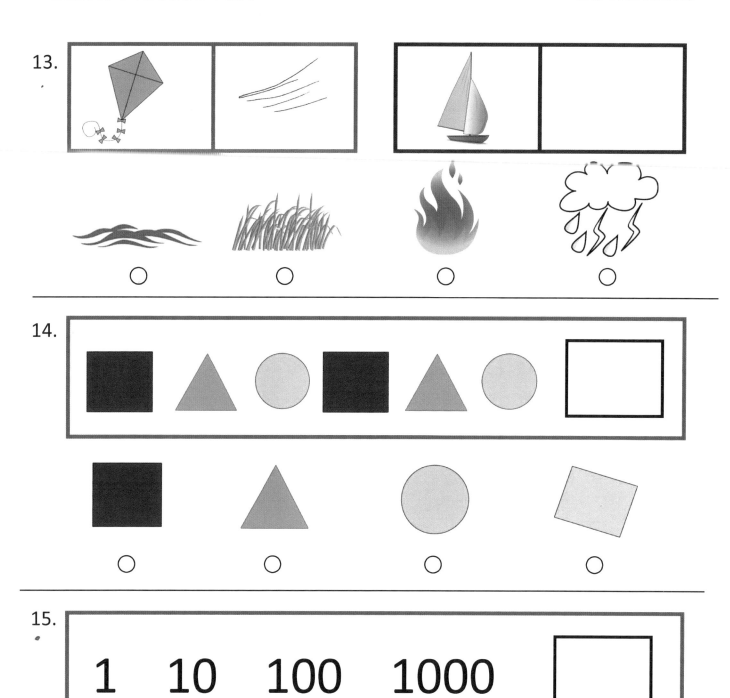

14.

15.

16.

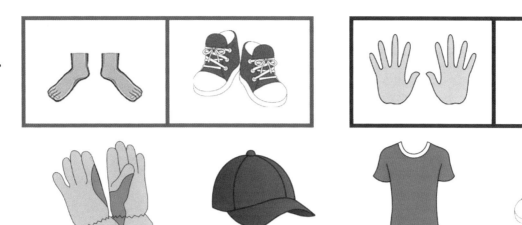

17.

18.

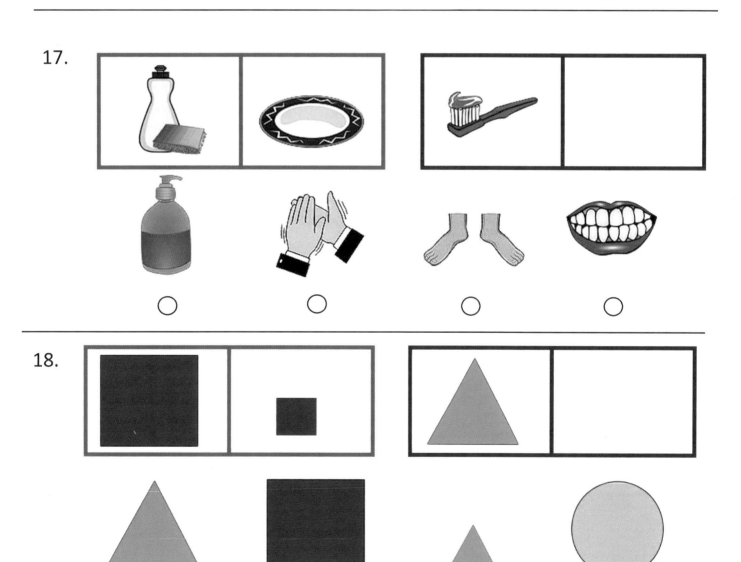

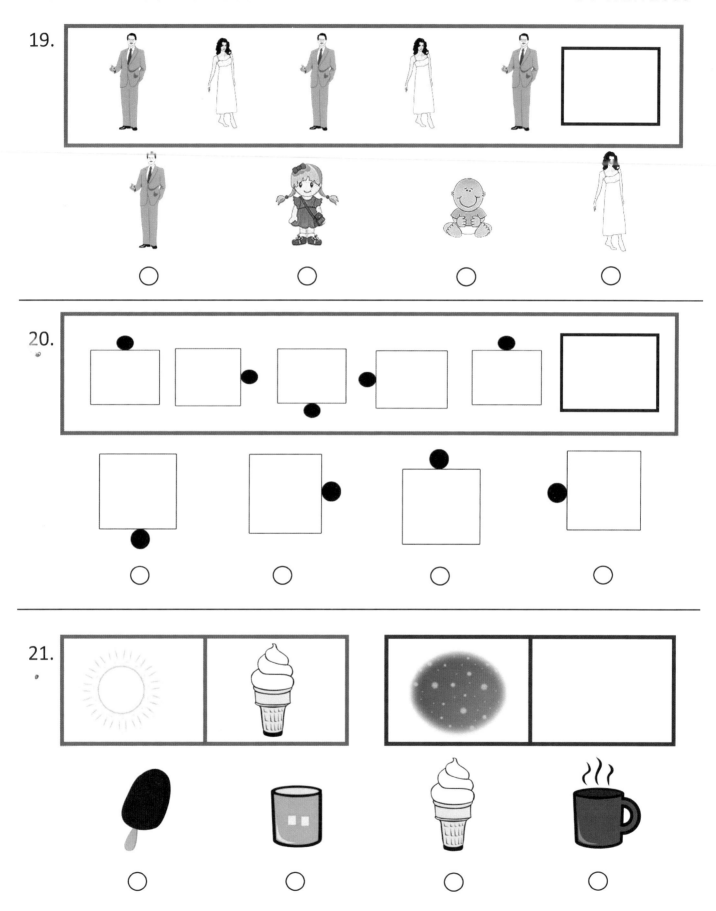

22.

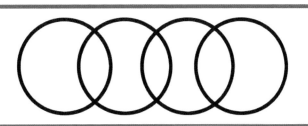

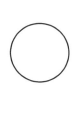 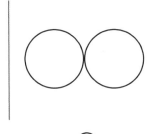 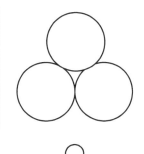 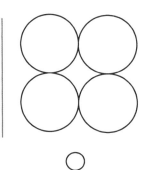

○   ○   ○   ○

23.

○   ○   ○   ○

24.

○   ○   ○   ○

25.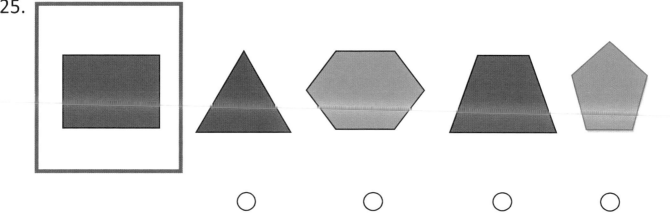

       ◯   ◯   ◯   ◯

26.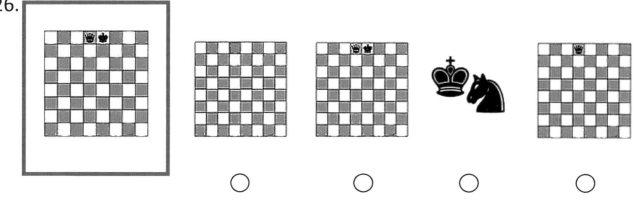

       ◯   ◯   ◯   ◯

27.

       ◯   ◯   ◯   ◯

28.

○   ○   ○   ○

29.

1. ×	1. ×	1. ✓	1. ✓
2. ×	2. ×	2. ✓	2. ✓
3. ×	3. ✓	3. ✓	3. ✓
4. ×	4. ✓	4. ✓	4. ✓
5. ×	5. ✓	5. ✓	5. ×

○   ○   ○   ○

30.

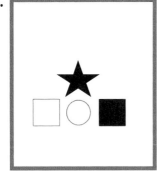  

○   ○   ○   ○

Answer Key for Topics 2 - 10

Topic	Page #	Question #	Answer
Topic 2	12	1	3
		2	4
		3	1
		4	2
	13	5	3
		6	1
		7	4
		8	2
	14	9	3
		10	4
		11	2
		12	1
	15	13	2
		14	1
		15	4
		16	3

Answer Key for Topic 2 - 10

Topic	Page #	Question #	Answer
	16	17	2
		18	3
		19	4
		20	1
	17	21	
	18	22	
	19	23	
	20	24	
Topic 3	21	1	2
		2	1
		3	4
	22	4	2
		5	3
		6	1
	23	7	2
		8	1

Answer Key for Topic 2 - 10

Topic	Page #	Question #	Answer
		9	1
	24	10	1
		11	3
		12	2
	25	13	3
		14	1
		15	3
	26	16	3
		17	3
		18	4
	27	19	2
		20	4
		21	3
	28	22	1
		23	2
		24	1

Answer Key for Topic 2 - 10

Topic	Page #	Question #	Answer
Topic 4	29	1	2
		2	1
		3	4
	30	4	2
		5	3
		6	3
	31	7	2
		8	3
		9	1
	32	10	2
		11	7
		12	3
	33	13	4
		14	5
		15	8
	34	16	1

 Gifted and Talented Test Prep 1   Jack and Jill Publishing Inc.

Answer Key for Topic 2 - 10

Topic	Page #	Question #	Answer
		17	7
		18	9
	35	19	2
		20	1
		21	5
	36	22	1
		23	2
		24	5
Topic 5	37	1	1&4
		2	2&5
		3	3&5
	38	4	1&4
		5	1&4
		6	2&4
	39	7	2&3
		8	1&4

Answer Key for Topic 2 - 10

Topic	Page #	Question #	Answer
		9	1&4
	40	10	Two bananas
		11	Red triangle
		12	Four leaves
	41	13	4
		14	2
		15	2
Topic 6	42	1	1
		2	2
		3	4
	43	4	1
		5	3
		6	3
	44	7	1
		8	2
		9	4

Gifted and Talented Test Prep 1 Jack and Jill Publishing Inc.

Answer Key for Topic 2 - 10

Topic	Page #	Question #	Answer
	45	10	
		11	
		12	
		13	
	46	14	
		15	
		16	
		17	
	47	18	
		19	
		20	
		21	
Topic 7	48	1	4
		2	4
		3	2
	49	4	3

Answer Key for Topic 2 - 10

Topic	Page #	Question #	Answer
		5	2
		6	1
	50	7	2
		8	1
		9	2
	51	10	4
		11	3
		12	3
	52	13	3
		14	3
		15	3
	53	16	2
		17	3
		18	1
	54	19	1
		20	3

Gifted and Talented Test Prep 1   Jack and Jill Publishing Inc.

Answer Key for Topic 2 - 10

Topic	Page #	Question #	Answer
		21	2
	55	22	2
		23	4
		24	1
Topic 8	56	1	3
		2	4
		3	2
	57	4	3
		5	3
		6	1
	58	7	3
		8	2
		9	1
	59	10	2
		11	4
		12	2

Answer Key for Topic 2 - 10

Topic	Page #	Question #	Answer
	60	13	3
		14	2
		15	3
	61	16	3
		17	4
		18	1
Topic 9	62	1	2
		2	2
		3	1
	63	4	3
		5	1
		6	2
	64	7	1
		8	2
		9	3
	65	10	1

    Gifted and Talented Test Prep 1   Jack and Jill Publishing Inc.

Answer Key for Topic 2 - 10

Topic	Page #	Question #	Answer
		11	3
		12	1
	66	13	1
		14	2
		15	3
	67	16	1
		17	1
		18	3
Topic 10	68	1	<table><tr><td>4</td><td>1</td></tr><tr><td>2</td><td>3</td></tr></table>
	69	2	<table><tr><td>1</td><td>2</td></tr><tr><td>4</td><td>3</td></tr></table>
	70	3	<table><tr><td>2</td><td>1</td></tr><tr><td>3</td><td>4</td></tr></table>
	71	4	<table><tr><td>2</td><td>1</td></tr><tr><td>3</td><td>4</td></tr></table>
	72	5	<table><tr><td>3</td><td>2</td></tr><tr><td>1</td><td>4</td></tr></table>

Answer Key for NNAT Exercise

Topic	Page #	Question #	Answer
NNAT EX.	74	1	2
		2	5
	75	3	5
		4	5
	76	5	4
		6	4
	77	7	5
		8	2
	78	9	3
		10	4
	79	11	2
		12	4
	80	13	4
		14	4
	81	15	2
		16	4

Gifted and Talented Test Prep 1   Jack and Jill Publishing Inc.

Answer Key for NNAT Exercise

Topic	Page #	Question #	Answer
NNAT EX.	82	17	2
		18	1
		19	2
	83	20	2
		21	4
		22	4
	84	23	2
		24	3
		25	3

49117856R00070

Made in the USA
Lexington, KY
26 January 2016